WHAT
Are robots made of ?

Om KIDZ
An imprint of Om Books International

Contents

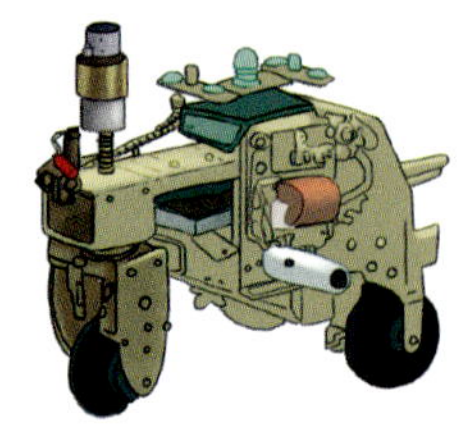

What is a robot?

A machine! A robot is a mechanical device that can carry out a variety of simple and complex actions on a command. It can also act according to instructions programmed in advance. Robots are designed by engineers to perform difficult tasks easily and with greater accuracy.

Find out

In which country can you find the most number of robots?

Pocket fact

Robota!
The word 'robot' comes from a Czech word 'robota', which means 'hard work or dull work'.

What can a robot do?

A lot of tasks! Robots can do many different kinds of jobs, like helping doctors perform delicate surgeries, assemble big cars and tiny computer chips. Robots are also sent deep into the ocean or into space to explore things.

What are the basic things a robot needs to work automatically?

Sensors, Actuators and Program! The sensors help a robot to perceive the world around it just like our sense organs (eyes, ears, nose, skin and tongue). The actuators help a robot to perform actions such as moving, making faces and making sounds. A program is a set of instructions that lets robots act on their own based on what it is sensing. A robot must have three essential parts- sensors, actuators and programs to work automatically.

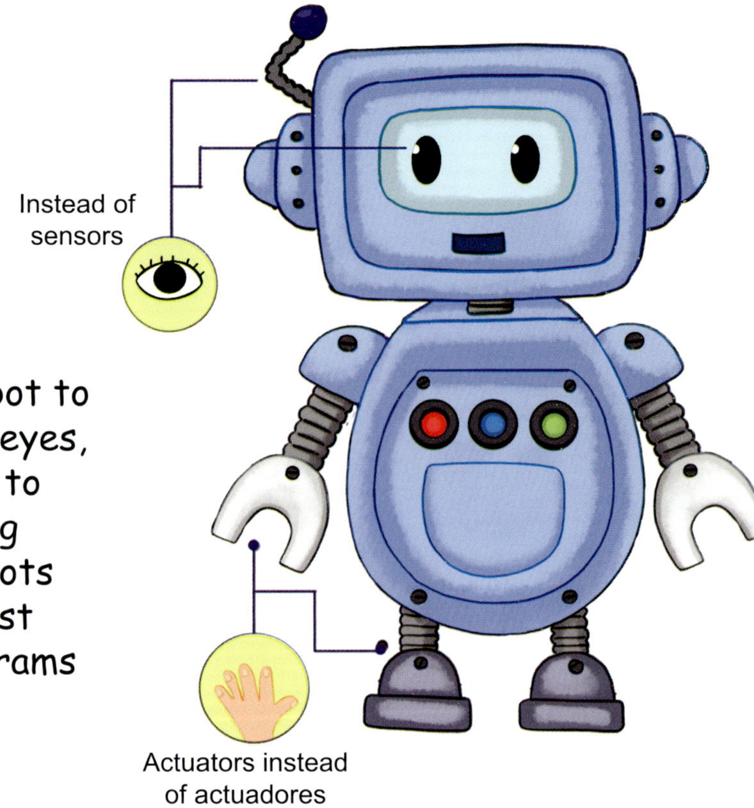

Find out

What is a controller in a robot?

Pocket fact

So many sensors!

A robot can have a number of sensors depending on the task it performs. These can be to detect colours, temperature, light and so on!

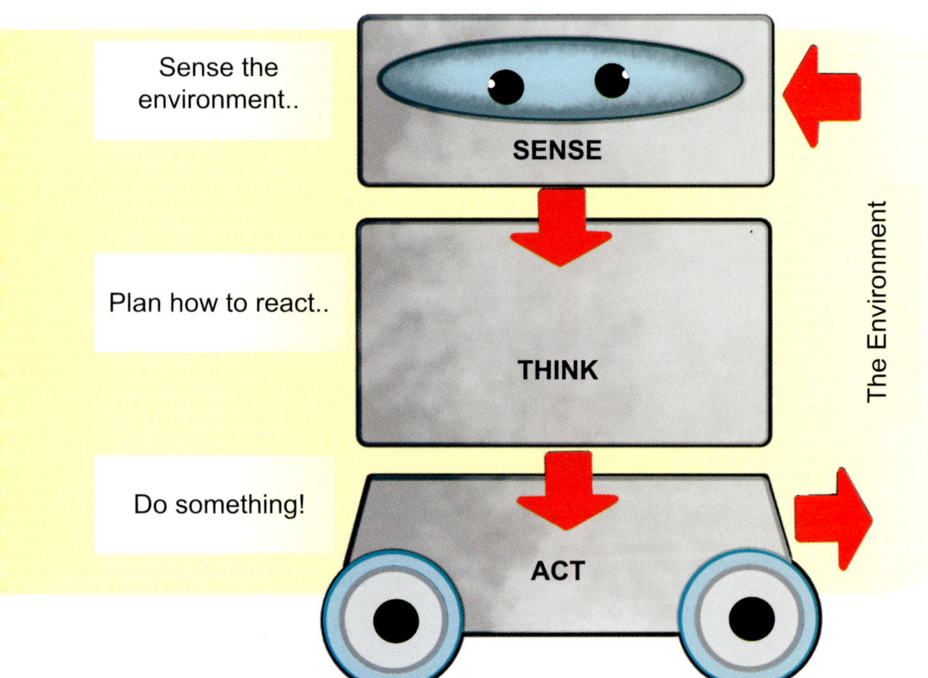

What is the Sense-Think-Act Cycle?

It is a decision-making process used by robots! A robot senses the world around it with the help of sensors. A robot cannot think like we do but its program helps it to plan how to react based on what it has sensed. Then the robot executes the action to be carried out i.e. it acts upon the world. This Sense-Think-Act Cycle is what makes robots different from other machines.

What are the different types of robots in use?

Many types! There are many ways we can define different types of robots. Based on their application and use, robots can be divided into eight types. These are industrial robots, domestic or household robots, medical robots, service robots, military robots, entertainment robots, space robots, and hobby and competition robots.

Pocket fact

Robots on Mars!

Two robots named Spirit and Opportunity were sent to Mars to explore the planet. They do much of their work alone, without commands from Earth because it takes a long time to send a signal from Earth to Mars.

Find out

What is the study of robots called?

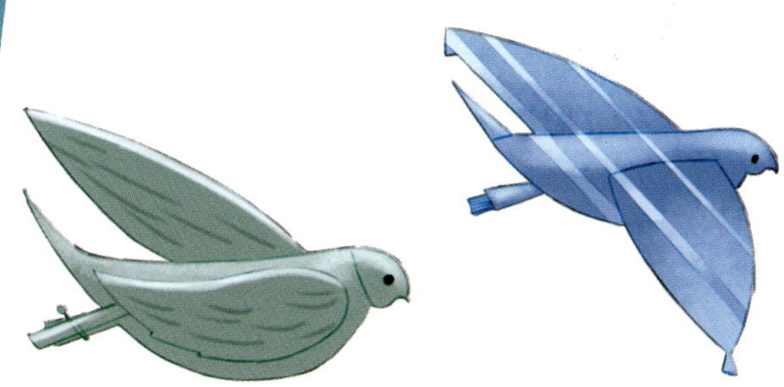

What was the first known robot?

It was a mechanical dove! Yes, the first robot did not look like complex machines or human-like robots. It was mechanical doves. It was created in the 5th century BCE by a Greek mathematician and astronomer Archytas. He made a wooden dove worked with the helped of compressed air or steam. The dove could fly hundreds of feet into the air while tethered to the ground.

What is a humanoid robot?

A humanoid robot is a robot that resembles a human being's body structure. Such a robot has a torso, a head, two arms and two legs. Some humanoids also have eyes and mouth. A humanoid robot helps us to perform human tasks like scientific research, entertainment, in mines, personal assistance and greeting guests and visitors.

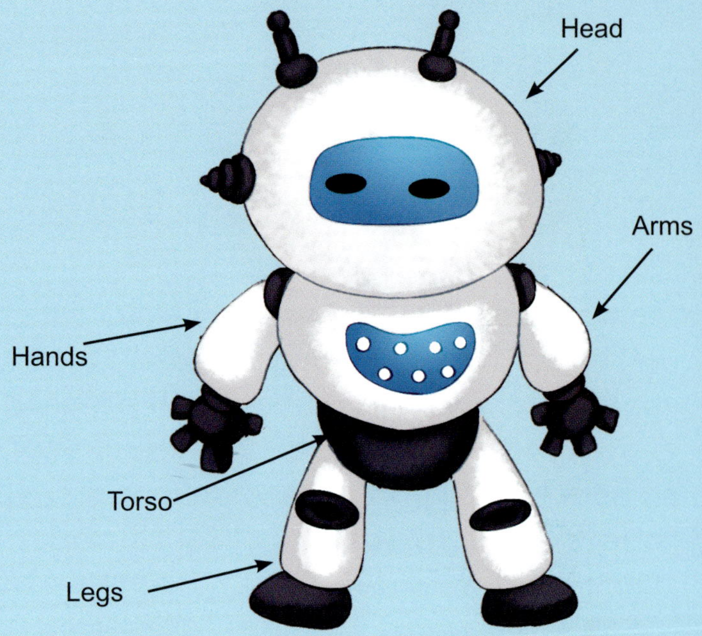

Find out

What does the word Android mean?

Pocket fact

The First Humanoid Design!
The first design of a humanoid robot was made by Leonardo da Vinci in the year 1495.

What is an Android robot?

An Android is a humanoid robot that looks and acts like a human. But it is different from a humanoid because it has a body with a flesh-like resemblance just as humans. Android robots can use machines, tools and infrastructure. They can perform many tasks that humans can do.

What is a robonaut?

It is a humanoid robot! A robonaut is a NASA robot. It is designed to work in space or in high risk environments. It is made up of a torso, two arms, a head and two legs with end effectors. Robonaut is currently operated inside the International Space Station.

Pocket fact

In 2000!
NASA started working on the Robonaut project in 1996. The first version of the robot was created in 2000.

Find out

What does 'nano' mean?

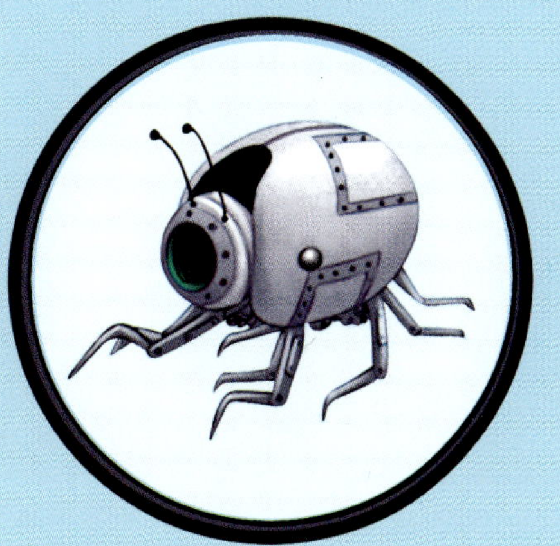

What is a nanobot?

A very tiny robot! A nanobot or a nanorobot is such a small robot that you need a microscope to see it. It is used to perform specific tasks repeatedly and with accuracy at very small dimensions. Nanorobots are still being developed. They would be of great help in performing delicate surgery.

What were some of the early robots?

They were automata-moving machines driven by water, air or clockwork! These automatic machines have been designed by inventors since ancient times. For example: mechanical doves, the elephant clock, Karakuri puppets. The elephant clock was designed by an Arab inventor al-Jazari in 1206. Karakuri puppets were mechanical dolls that could act out stories at the theatre.

Find out

What does the word 'Karakuri' mean?

Pocket fact

Electric Teeth!

The robot Eric could make blue sparks from its teeth by using electricity.

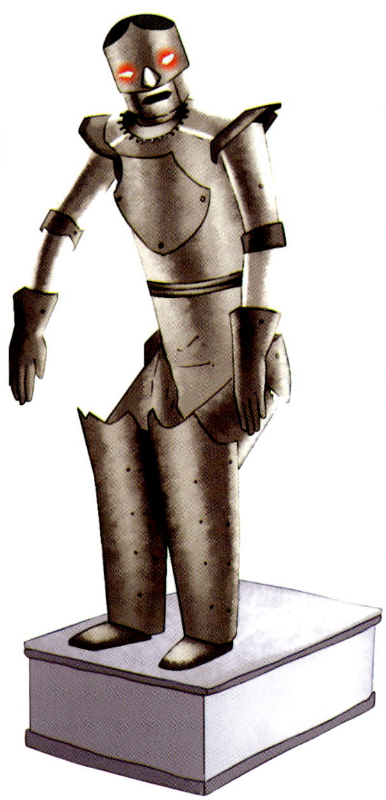

What was the first human-shaped robot?

It was called Eric! Eric was the first British robot built in 1928. It was 7 feet tall and had armour that made it look like a knight. The inside of its body had many wires connected to motors. The wires helped it do different actions like stand, sit, turn left and right and wave its arms. Though Eric was able to sit and stand, it could not move its legs to walk.

What were the first robots to make their own decisions?

They were two tortoises! An American scientist William Grey Walter designed two robot tortoises named Elmer and Elsie. They could react to their surroundings like real animals and make their own decisions.

Find out

In which year were Elmer and Elsie created?

Pocket fact

Shakey was named so because it was tall and had a tendency to shake!

What was the first robot that was able to think for itself?

It was called Shakey! Shakey was the first general-purpose mobile robot that could think for itself. It was developed at the Standford Research Institute, California. Shakey was a tall robot with an antenna for a radio link, sonar range finders, a television camera and bump detectors. It could look around a room using its camera and plan how to move without bumping into things using its bump detectors.

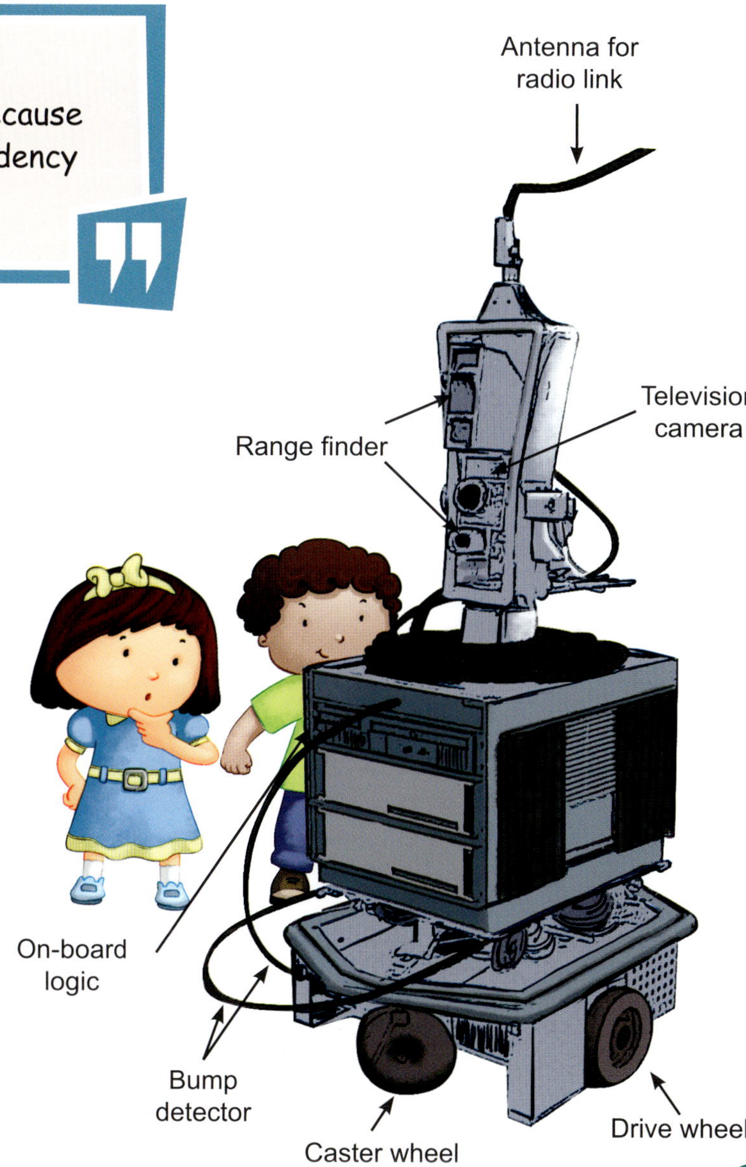

What is a Nao?

A robot that plays soccer and does lots more! Nao is a friendly human-like robot that was developed in France. It is a smart interactive robot that was programmed by roboticists to walk, talk and play RoboCup soccer! Robo has been continually been evolving since its invention. It can welcome guests and provide information in a variety of languages when placed at hotels!

Pocket fact

Robots at the Show!
The first show in the world with robots in the starring roles was held in 2013. NAO was a part of this "ROBOTS" show and charmed the audience.

Try this

In which year was SAFFIR invented?

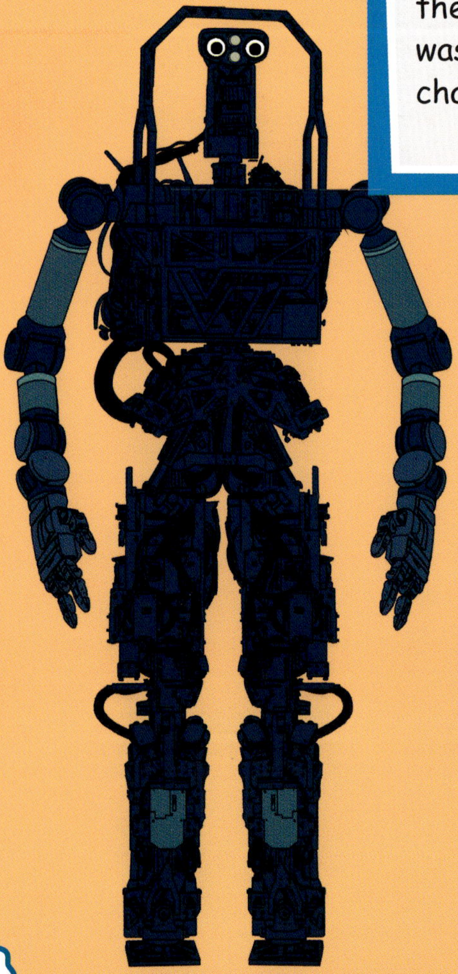

What kind of robot is a SAFFIR?

A fire-fighting robot! SAFFIR was developed by TREC (a technology company in Virginia) and the U.S. Navy. It can see through smoke. Its main purpose is to assist sailors in fighting fires, controlling damage and carrying out inspections onboard ships.

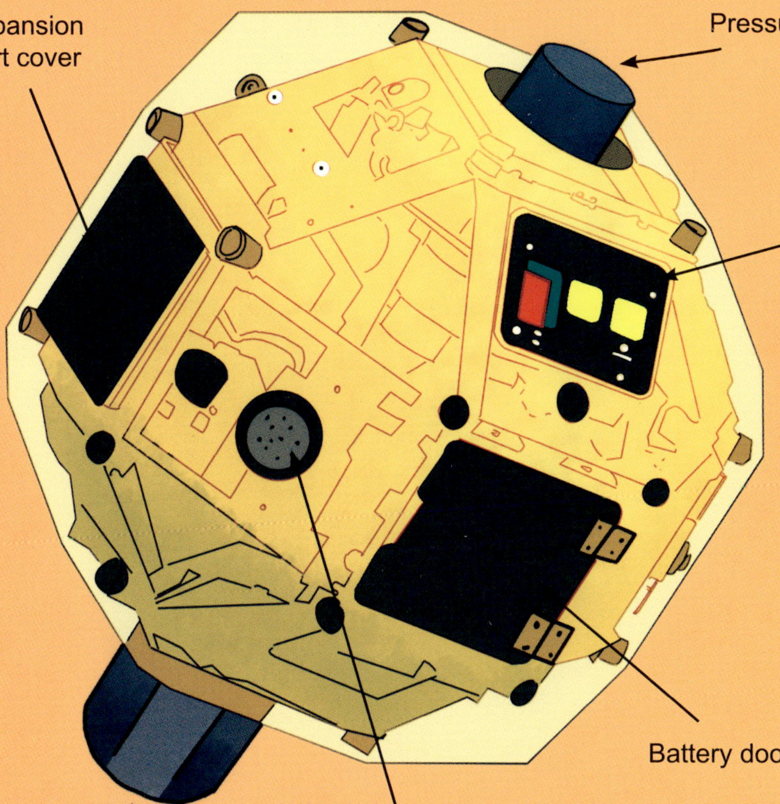

What work do SPHERES robots do?

They help astronauts in space! SPHERES are robots in the shape of spherical satellites that are free flying. SPHERES are used inside the International Space Station. They help in testing instructions for spacecraft that perform automated tasks.

Pocket fact

SPHERES robots are also used by students at Robotics competitions.

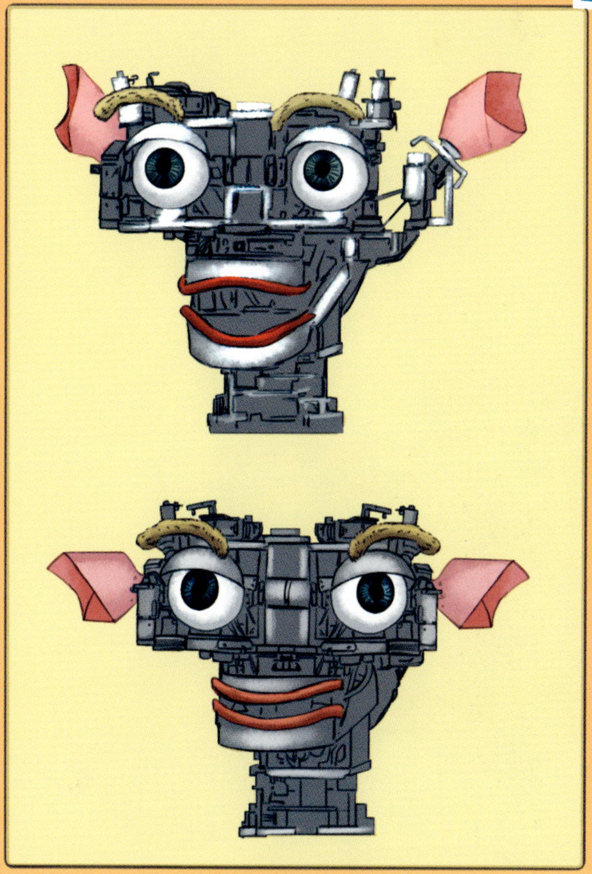

What are the special features of the KISMET robot?

It is an expressive robot that was designed to relate to people and learn from them. It was developed in the United States in late 1990s. KISMET has learnt about feelings. It can make faces to express happiness, sadness or surprise!

Find out

Can the KISMET robot speak?

What is a tracked robot?

A robot that moves on tracks instead of wheels! Robots with tracks are suitable for moving across uneven surfaces. They can move on ice, mud and even snow! Robots with track are designed to fight fires and travel in space.

Find out

What are caterpillar tracks?.

Flipper arms!

Tracked robots may also have flipper arms. They use these arms to climb stairs or obstacles that are a lot taller than them.

What are wheeled robots?

Robots that use wheels to move! Robots with wheels are fast to move, easier to build and program. They are also better controlled than other types of robots. But such robots can trip over bumpy ground. Robots with wheels are used to mow lawns, guard prisons and carry materials inside factories and hospitals.

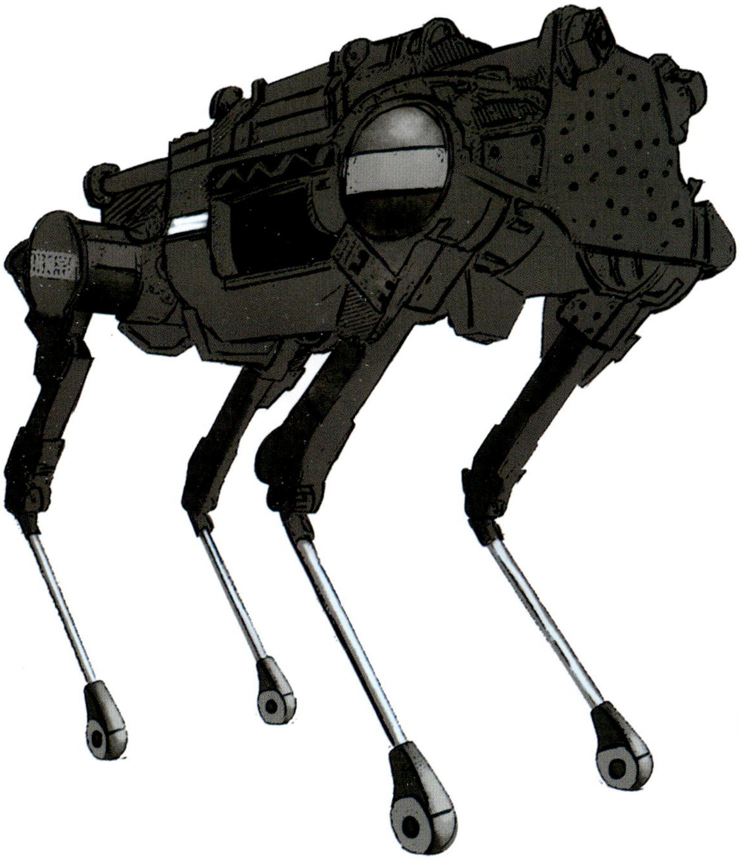

What are legged robots used for?

Legged robots are robots that use limbs to move around. They resemble humans or insects. Robots with legs are suitable to climb up walls or step over objects. Such robots are used in jobs like cleaning up chemical spills or exploring uneven surface of the ocean floor.

Find out

In which year was the Handle robot built?

The Big Dog!

The Big Dog is a four-legged robot that resembles a mule. It was created to help soldiers where vehicles can't be used to carry loads.

What are hybrid robots?

Robots that have both legs and wheels are called hybrid robots. Such robots can move fast because of wheels as well as walk and climb with their legs. The robot Handle built by a company called Boston Dynamics, is an example of a hybrid robot.

What is a snakebot?

It's a robot in the form of a snake! A robotic snake or snakebot moves from side to side like a snake. It has tiny cameras along its body to help us monitor what the robot snake sees. Such robots can climb trees and swim. They can be used to move through collapsed buildings after an earthquake where people can't enter.

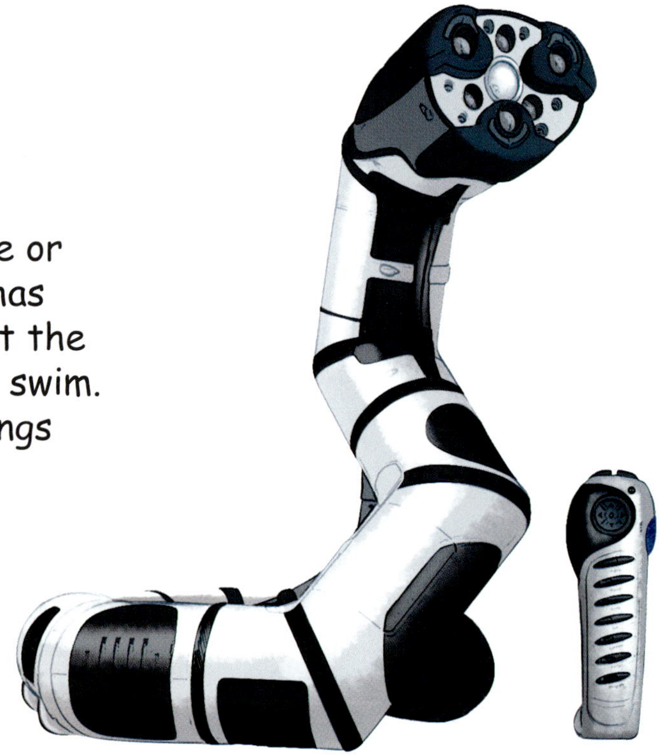

Find out

How much does the Cyro weigh?

What kind of robot is Cyro?

A robot that resembles a jellyfish! Cyro was built by the U.S. Navy. It is the size of a beach umbrella, approximately 5.7 feet long. Cyro has a jelly-fish like dome and eight metal arms. It can be used to keep a watch over the ocean, make maps of the ocean floor and study life under water.

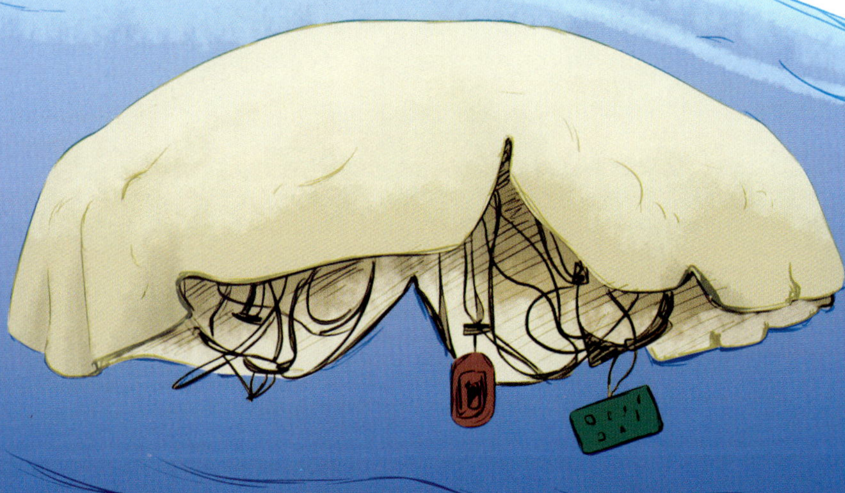

Pocket fact

The word "Cyro" comes from the Latin name of Jelly Fish, cyanea capillata.

What kind of a robot is a Robear?

It is a nursing robot! The Robear is a Japanese robot that helps elderly people or patients to sit and stand. It is said to be a "strong robot with the gentle touch" because it is strong enough to lift a person and supports them with care.

RIBA

The first model of Robear was announced in 2009. It was called RIBA and later renamed to Robear.

Find out

How are robots used by doctors?

What makes robots useful workers?

Robots can be wonderful workers because they can be used in different environments like blistering heat, freezing cold or places that are dirty! They can also explore volcanoes or be sent to far away planets where human beings cannot reach. Robots can work for days without being tired or bored!

Index

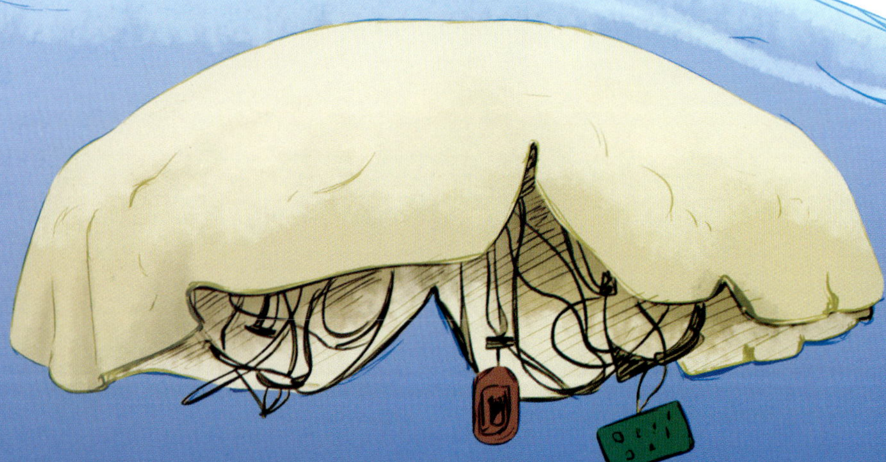